Adventures of the Early Church

By KATHLEEN M. ZAFFORE

Illustrated by NORMAN SEARS

ACCENT PUBLICATIONS
DENVER

Accent Publications, Inc.
12100 W. Sixth Avenue
P. O. Box 15337
Denver, Colorado 80215

Copyright ©1984 Accent Publications, Inc.
Printed in the United States of America

All rights reserved. No portion of this book may be reproduced in any form without the written permission of the publishers, with the exception of brief exerpts in magazine reviews.

ISBN 0-89636-118-7

Contents

1. A Promise and a Command 1
2. The Holy Spirit Comes 6
3. The Attack Begins 10
4. Deadly Lies 18
5. A Face Like an Angel's 24
6. The Magician's Silver 30
7. Blinded by the Light! 35
8. Escape Through the Wall 41
9. A Message in a Bundle 47
10. Something Missing Is Found 51
11. Break Out 56
12. The First Missionaries 63
13. Earthquake in Philippi 68
14. Paul Imprisoned 74
15. Shipwreck! 79
16. Rome at Last 87

1. A Promise and a Command

Peter hurried, gulping down the last bite of his breakfast. The sun was already rising and Jesus had told His disciples to be on time today. Something important was going to happen. Peter strapped on his sandals and leaped down the stairs in three long strides.

"Good morning, Peter! I'm glad to see that you're up and at 'em," John greeted him happily. "Let's get going. I'm anxious to hear what Jesus has to tell us today."

"Me too," Peter replied, catching his breath. "Do you think that Jesus is ready to unite Israel again

Story based on Acts 1:1-26

and be the King? I wonder what He'll have each of us do when He wins the throne?"

John shrugged his shoulders and stepped up the pace. "Don't worry about it, Peter," he advised. "Jesus will tell you what He wants you to do."

Jesus had walked out of His tomb forty days before, victorious over death. And since then, He had been meeting often with His special disciples, teaching them about the kingdom of God.

Jesus had performed mighty miracles during the past three years, but what He was able to do in His resurrected body left no room for anybody to doubt that He was truly God's Son. He appeared and disappeared when He wished. He even walked through locked doors. The disciples thought that nothing—not even the powerful Roman army—could stop Jesus from becoming the King of Israel.

The Jewish people were tired of having Roman soldiers marching in their streets, and Roman governors telling them what they could and couldn't do. The disciples could hardly wait for Jesus to establish His kingdom and kick the Romans out of Palestine.

Peter and John jogged breathlessly up the Mount of Olives outside Jerusalem. Jesus was already there, surrounded by the other nine disciples. He smiled at Peter and John as they joined the group.

"I am glad to have you all with me on this important day," Jesus said.

"Lord!" Peter blurted out. He was so excited that he just couldn't hold still. "Are you going to seize the throne now and become the King of Israel? We're ready to fight beside You." The other disciples agreed with a cheer.

"Only the Father knows when that will happen," Jesus answered calmly, "and now is not the time."

The disciples gasped and looked at each other with shock and confusion. "Jesus is not going to be King?" someone whispered. "How can that be?"

Jesus' eyes moved from face to face and He announced, "I have some important work for you to do. You are my apostles and I have chosen you to go out and be my witnesses. But first, you must return to Jerusalem and wait there."

"Why, Lord?" Peter asked.

"I promise you," said Jesus, "that very soon the Father will send His powerful Spirit to live in each one of you. When that happens, you must start here in Jerusalem to tell everyone about me and my work. Then you will go out into the countryside of Judea and Samaria spreading the Word, until the whole world knows who I am."

As Jesus finished speaking, He began to slowly rise up in the air. Peter's mouth fell open at the sight. Jesus disappeared into the clouds and Peter realized that his Lord was returning to Heaven. All the apostles stood on the windy hilltop gazing into the sky for a long, long time, hoping to catch one last glimpse of Jesus.

"You men of Galilee!" A strong voice broke the silence and startled Peter. He quickly looked in the direction of the voice and blinked his eyes a couple of times to make sure that he wasn't seeing things. Two men dressed in brilliant white robes had suddenly appeared on the hill. Angels, Peter guessed excitedly.

"Why are you men standing here staring up at the clouds?" one of the men asked. "Don't worry, Jesus will return one day the same way you saw Him go into Heaven. He hasn't left you forever."

John turned to the other apostles and said, "These men are right. There's no sense in standing out here all day feeling sad. Let's do what Jesus told us to do—head back to Jerusalem and wait. After all, He didn't leave us alone, because the Holy Spirit will come soon. Right?" He looked around to ask the white-robed men, but they were gone.

When the apostles arrived in the city, they gathered at the house where they usually met, and climbed up the stairs to a large room. For several days people gathered there to pray with them.

There were only eleven apostles now, because Judas Iscariot, the disciple who had betrayed Jesus, was dead. Peter and John, James and Andrew, Philip, Thomas, Nathanael, Matthew, James the Less, Simon the Zealot, and the other Judas were the eleven. Peter reminded them that they must pick someone to take Judas' place. "The Scriptures say in Psalms that we will do this," he said.

The apostles picked two men and prayed to God to help them choose the right one. They drew straws and a man named Matthias became the twelfth apostle.

Then the Christians settled down to wait, but the Holy Spirit did not keep them waiting for long.

2. The Holy Spirit Comes

Every day for ten days, the apostles met in the upstairs room to wait for the Holy Spirit and to pray with other men and women who believed that Jesus was the Son of God.

Finally it was Pentecost, the Jewish Thanksgiving. On that day the apostles and the other believers met as usual. Peter was walking around the room greeting everyone when suddenly a thunderous sound as of wind was heard outside the house and howled into the room where they were meeting.

The roaring sound filled the room. And little

tongues like fire appeared upon every person. The apostles knew in a flash what was happening. The promised Holy Spirit had come.

The news spread all over Jerusalem and people raced to the apostles' house to find out what was happening. The curious crowd surrounded the house. There were religious Jews from Egypt and Rome and Libya, and many other faraway nations. And they were all struggling to get a look at the strange goings-on in the noisy house.

Peter and the other apostles saw the crowd gathering. They hurried outside and began to walk through the packed street, speaking. The people in the crowd were stunned. Each one was hearing from the apostles all about the mighty works of God—in his very own language.

"What's happening here?" called one man from the crowd. "Aren't you from Galilee? It's impossible for you to be speaking so many foreign languages."

Another man yelled, "Oh, they're all drunk."

Peter boldly stepped out of the group of apostles and called to the crowd, "Listen, everyone. These men couldn't be drunk. It's only nine o'clock in the morning. But you are seeing what God promised to His prophet Joel in the Scriptures. He said,

> 'In the last days I will pour out my Spirit. And I will show wonders in the heaven above and signs in the earth beneath before the day of the Lord comes. And it shall be that whoever calls on the name of the Lord shall be saved.' "

Peter had never been to school to learn how to speak so powerfully before crowds of people. In fact, he was a little shocked by his own courage. After all, he was only a fisherman.

He paused for a moment and realized that the crowd had gotten quiet. The people were listening, and the Holy Spirit had much to tell them through Peter. Suddenly Peter understood what Jesus wanted him to do.

"You all remember Jesus of Nazareth, don't you?" he shouted. "He performed mighty works and wonders and signs, like healing the lame and making the blind see. Jesus did these things with the power of God. You all saw those miracles.

"Well, God knew long ago what you would do to Jesus, and He allowed you and the Romans to crucify Him. But the tomb wasn't strong enough to hold Jesus. God raised Him up from death and we here are all witnesses that Jesus is alive. He's now sitting at the right hand of the Father in Heaven. Hear me now. God has made Jesus, whom you crucified, both Lord and Messiah of Israel."

"Oh, no!" people in the crowd cried out. "What have we done?" They were saddened by what Peter told them. And they were scared for having had a part in killing the Son of God.

"What can we do to keep God from being angry with us?" they asked the apostles.

Peter answered, "Repent and ask God to forgive you. Then be baptized in the name of Jesus Christ, and He will give you the gift of the Holy Spirit."

People all around Peter began falling to their knees, praying for God to forgive them. Nearly 3,000 people believed that day. The word about Jesus spread throughout Jerusalem. And many more people believed that He was indeed the Messiah who was promised by the prophets in the old Scriptures.

The early church was off to a great start.

3. The Attack Begins

Caiaphas looked out his window one day at Jerusalem. He was not happy about what was going on all over the city.

"Here I am, a chief priest, and I can't figure out how to stop these people who are telling everyone that Jesus is the Son of God," he thought angrily. "But what's worse, they're pointing their fingers at me and the other leaders saying that we're responsible for Jesus' death. And the people are listening. If we don't do something to end this nonsense soon, the people might rebel against us." He straightened his priestly robes and stormed out

Story based on Acts 3:1—5:42

of his house. "These Jesus preachers are wrecking my life."

When Caiaphas walked through the Beautiful Gate of the temple, people were already gathering to listen to the apostles. He stopped dead in his tracks. There, at the Beautiful Gate, stood Peter and John talking to the crippled man who had been coming there for years to beg for coins.

"What are they up to?" Caiaphas wondered, sneaking through the crowd to get a better look. Caiaphas was only a few feet away when he saw an amazing sight.

"In the name of Jesus Christ," Peter was saying to the man, "walk." The crippled man stood up and walked around, staring at his healed legs. Then, with a shout of joy, he started leaping and praising God.

Caiaphas was stunned. If he hadn't seen the healing with his own eyes, he wouldn't have believed it. He followed the crowd around Peter to Solomon's Porch.

Peter quieted the awestruck crowd by saying, "Don't be so surprised. We didn't make this crippled man walk. We don't have that kind of power in ourselves. But God does have power and He gave it to His Son Jesus. It is by the name of

Jesus that this man can now walk."

Several priests and the captain of the temple guards had joined Caiaphas on the edge of the crowd.

"What's going on?" they asked him, straining to see over the heads of the people.

"That preacher is explaining that it was through Jesus that he healed the crippled beggar," Caiaphas whispered.

"What?" the captain exclaimed.

Caiaphas shook his head, puzzled. "I saw it happen."

Peter was shouting to the crowd. "Turn away from your sins. We know that you and the rulers killed Jesus because you didn't understand who He was. Now God has raised Him from death in order to bless you."

"That's it!" Caiaphas turned to the captain. "Arrest him for teaching that Jesus was raised from the dead."

The captain signaled to the guards. They broke through the crowd and grabbed Peter and John. People shouted and scattered as the guards dragged them off. The two apostles were thrown into jail for the night.

But Caiaphas had John and Peter arrested too

late. Many more people in the crowd had turned to Jesus that day.

Bright and early in the morning, John and Peter were brought before the Council of the Jews. Caiaphas grinned happily. Now he had them. He was sure that the council would find them guilty of *something*. If these two ringleaders were tossed into prison, maybe the people of Jerusalem would forget all about them and Jesus.

"How did you heal that man?" Annas, the high priest, asked.

"By the name of Jesus Christ, the One whom you crucified and who conquered death by God's power. Jesus is the only One who can give you salvation," Peter answered with a bold voice.

The men of the council looked at each other nervously. "What can we do?" they asked each other. "We can't deny that a miracle happened, because everyone has seen the crippled man walking around."

"Let's warn them to stop preaching about Jesus," Annas suggested. "Tell them we'll have to punish them harshly. After all, we don't want these rebellious ideas to spread any farther."

But Peter replied, "Should we obey you or God? We have to tell people about Jesus."

"If you do," Annas said, "something terrible is bound to happen to you." And then the apostles were set free. Immediately Peter and John met with other believers and told them what had happened.

"We must pray," Peter said. "Pray that God will make us strong enough not to be afraid of these threats against us." And as soon as they said "Amen," the place where they were meeting began to shake, just like in an earthquake. The Holy Spirit was busy again. Everyone began to speak bravely about God, and they knew that their prayer had been answered.

These believers were going to need all the strength and courage God gave them at the prayer meeting.

* * * * *

For a little while, the council didn't bother the church, and the church continued to grow. Everyone knew that Peter was a man of God and many came to him to be healed. People even put their sick friends and relatives out into the street hoping that Peter's shadow would fall on them, causing them to be cured.

Everywhere Caiaphas and Annas went, they heard, "Jesus this and Peter that." They never heard compliments about the council anymore. "These Jesus preachers are ruining us," they agreed. Along with the other Jewish leaders, they had the apostles arrested again.

The prison door slammed behind them with a loud bang, and darkness surrounded them in the musty cell. All night they took turns praying, and suddenly an eerie light began to glow in one corner.

"Look!" John whispered, standing up and pulling Peter to his feet. In the light stood a man. The man motioned for the apostles to come to the door—and it opened. Peter rubbed his eyes to make sure he wasn't just dreaming. But sure enough, the heavy wooden door stood open.

"Go on out," the angel urged. "You must return to the temple and continue to tell everyone about the life they can have in Jesus."

The angel went with them through the prison. And not one guard noticed that the apostles were escaping. When the sun came up, the apostles entered the temple and started teaching again.

Early in the morning the council met and asked the guards to bring the prisoners to them. But when the guards opened the heavy locked door, they gasped with surprise. The cell was empty.

"We don't know what happened," they reported to the rulers. "The door was locked and there were guards stationed by the cell all night. Somehow those men got out."

"And they're at Solomon's Porch preaching again," a man shouted, racing into the council out of breath.

"Go get them!" Annas ordered the captain of the guards. The captain could hardly believe that anyone could have escaped from his prison, but there at Solomon's Porch were the apostles, surrounded by hundreds of people.

"Don't rush in at them," the captain advised the guards. "We don't want to start a riot." So the guards went to the apostles quietly, and took all twelve to the council.

"We warned you," Annas shouted. "You were not to teach about Jesus anymore, but you went against us. You even accused us of killing Him."

Peter replied, "We told you that we must obey God, not you. After all, it is God who forgives our sins through Jesus, not you." Peter never missed a chance to tell about his Lord.

Annas was so angry that he nearly exploded, but God had the situation under control. A highly respected member of the council, named Gamaliel, calmed everyone and had the apostles wait outside.

"Men of Israel," Gamaliel told the council, "think about what you're doing. If these men are following their own plans, their church will fade away. And if they are truly following God's plans, nothing you do can stop them."

"That makes sense," Annas agreed. But the council decided to teach the apostles a lesson by having them beaten before letting them go again. "And don't teach about Jesus ever again," Annas ordered.

Peter and the others left the council. Their backs were cut open and bleeding from the sharp whip lashes they had received. But they were happy. Even the cruel whipping couldn't shake the apostles' belief in Jesus. They returned to the temple as soon as they were well and never stopped telling the crowds about their Lord Jesus.

But the worst was yet to come.

4. Deadly Lies

The house where the believers had been meeting was too small to hold the whole church. So the apostles moved the meeting place to the side of the temple called Solomon's Porch.

The believers enjoyed getting together every day at Solomon's Porch. No one had to drag them out of bed or beg them to go up to the temple. Rich and poor, old and young, they loved Jesus and were excited about gathering together. They visited with each other, sharing what God had done for them. And every day they listened to the apostles preach the good news about God's free gift of eternal life through Jesus.

If a brother needed food or clothing or a place to stay, all he had to do was tell the apostles. He would get what he needed right away, because the believers showered the apostles with money and food to take care of the poor.

Joseph Barnabas loved his brothers and sisters in Jesus. And he was concerned that many of them didn't have enough to eat or that they had worn-out sandals.

"God has blessed me with a good field," he thought. "The field produces grains and fruits that the poor could eat. But my field is in another country so I can't get the food to the poor before it spoils." Joseph decided to sell the field, and when he received the money for it he took the coins straight to the apostles.

He laid the bag of money at Peter's feet, and said, "I want this money to go to the poor. But I don't know what everyone needs as well as you do, so I'd like you to give it away for me."

"God bless you, Barnabas," Peter said, hugging his friend. "I know that you love Jesus because you care so much about other people. Thank you for your gift."

But not all the people who gathered every day at

the temple were as loving as Joseph Barnabas. One man lurked in the shadows, watching Peter accept the bag of coins from Barnabas.

"Peter never pays attention to me," the man, Ananias, grumbled to himself. "I want to be a popular leader in the church, just like Barnabas, but how . . ." Suddenly Ananias snapped his fingers and grinned. "I've got it!" he thought. And quietly he slipped away from Solomon's Porch to carry out his plan.

Later that afternoon, Ananias rushed into his house and called his wife. "Sapphira! Sapphira! I've got news. Come quickly!"

Sapphira hurried into the room, wondering what on earth Ananias could be so excited about. "Now, what?" she questioned him. She was used to his schemes to become rich and famous, and she figured that he had been out all day working on some new plan. Lately he had been trying to figure out some way to become an important person up at the temple with the Jesus believers.

"I've come up with a foolproof plan to get the apostles to like us," he said.

"I suppose you want me to bake bread for the poor or something," Sapphira frowned, "and let you take all the credit."

"No, no! Nothing like that," Ananias said. "You don't have to do anything except back up my story. You see, I sold that extra field of ours today. You know the one we always have trouble renting out? Look!" And he dumped a large pile of coins on the table.

Sapphira's eyes bulged out of her head. "How did you get so much money for that poor field?"

Well, I stretched the truth a little," her husband confessed. "But the important thing is that we have the money, and now we'll give it to Peter for the poor. Then everyone will be glad to have us around."

"Are you crazy?" Sapphira demanded, fingering the coins. "You don't really want to give all of this money away, do you?"

Ananias smiled wickedly. "Of course not! We won't give it all away. We'll just *say* we are giving it all. No one will ever know, except us."

The next morning, Ananias counted out the coins and put them into two piles. He placed the smaller pile in the bag, kissed Sapphira good-bye, and headed toward the temple.

Ananias waited until Peter was quieting the crowd so that he could speak. Then, in a loud voice, Ananias announced, "I have sold a field, and I brought all the money to you to be given to the poor." And he laid the bag of coins at Peter's feet.

Ananias stood there, smiling, waiting for his reward from the apostles. But instead, he saw that Peter was frowning angrily.

"Why are you lying to the Holy Spirit?" Peter demanded. Ananias sputtered and took a step away from the apostle. "How did Peter find out?" he wondered fearfully.

"You didn't have to give us all the money from the sale. For that matter, you didn't need to give us any of the money. You could have kept it all for yourself. But now, what you've done is worse than just being selfish," Peter exclaimed. "You haven't told the truth about this gift. Don't you realize that you aren't lying to us? You are lying to God."

Terrible fear swept through Ananias' body, but it was too late to be sorry. He gasped, and fell to the floor—dead.

Whispered voices circled the crowd, while several young men carried Ananias' body away to be buried.

Sapphira waited and waited for Ananias to come home and tell her how his plan had worked.

Three hours later, he still hadn't shown up. Her curiosity got the better of her, and she walked up to the temple to see what was going on.

As she wandered through the crowd, people pointed at her and whispered, "There goes the wife of Ananias." She smiled because she was glad to be recognized. She broke through the front of the crowd and Peter saw her and called to her.

"Sapphira," Peter asked, pointing to the bag of coins still lying on the ground, "is this all the money from the sale of your field?"

Sapphira recognized the money bag and answered, "Yes."

Peter shook his head at her sadly and said, "I can't understand why you and your husband decided that you could lie to God and get away with it. Look over there. Those young men just buried your husband, and now they will bury you." At those words, Sapphira also fell down dead.

"Did you see that?" people asked each other with fear. "It doesn't pay to lie to God."

Every day more and more people believed in Jesus, God's Son, and the church continued to grow. But some people were angry about Jesus' church, and they were willing to do anything to destroy it.

5. A Face Like an Angel's

The church in Jerusalem continued growing by leaps and bounds, and the apostles became busier every day taking care of the needs of believers.

Late one afternoon, Peter returned exhausted from his rounds of the city. John and James were walking up the street from the opposite direction, also looking beat. The three sat down in the shade of the house to wait for the other apostles to get back.

"We were supposed to meet here hours ago to pray," Peter sighed.

"Did you teach at the temple today?" John

Story based on Acts 6:1—8:4

asked, rubbing his tired legs.

"Of course," Peter answered, "but I couldn't stay long because of the load of food and clothing I had to deliver to the poor. Don't get me wrong. I'm not complaining. I'm glad that everyone is so generous. It takes all day to hand out everything they give us. But we twelve aren't getting our work done."

John nodded, "I've heard some complaints, too, that we're forgetting to give food to some of the widows. As busy as we are, I suppose that is possible."

"Maybe it's time for us to spread some of our work load to other men," James suggested, "so that we can do our jobs—praying and teaching."

John and Peter gladly agreed. When all the apostles gathered that evening, they prayed about how they should select the men for these important jobs. They decided that the people in the church should do the choosing.

The believers chose seven men who were wise and good and filled with the Holy Spirit, and called them deacons. Stephen was one of these men.

It was easy to understand why Stephen was chosen. He loved Jesus with all of his heart, and he wasn't afraid to tell anyone about Him. Stephen even performed miracles in Jesus' name. He was becoming a pretty popular person, and that made several wicked men jealous.

"Stephen," the men said with evil smiles, "explain to us how this Jesus of yours is greater than Moses who gave us the Law." They hoped to make Stephen look stupid. But by the time Stephen had finished answering, the men who had questioned him were the ones who looked dumb.

The men met secretly to plot against Stephen. "He made us look like fools today," they complained to each other. "We can't let him get away with that." They agreed to pay off other men to tell lies about Stephen.

The false rumors about the deacon spread like wildfire. And before long, people all over Jerusalem were whispering, "Have you heard that Stephen speaks against God and Moses?" Eventually, the council leaders heard the rumors and were only too glad to arrest him as a follower of Jesus.

Stephen was brought before the council. The men who had been paid to lie about him came. "That's him," they said. "He's the one who says that Jesus will tear down the temple and will change all of the laws that Moses gave us."

If you wanted to make the Jewish leaders angry, all you had to do was put down the temple and the laws of Moses. The members of the council frowned at Stephen. The deacon was in a lot of trouble, but he didn't look worried at all. In fact, as the leaders stared at him angrily, they noticed that his face was as strong and as peaceful as the face of an angel.

Annas pointed his finger at Stephen. "Are these men telling the truth about you?"

Stephen looked around at the furious faces and knew that these men were not ready to believe the truth. Then he began to speak bravely. "Don't you realize that God is greater than the temple? He could never live inside that little building, but He can live in every heart. You all are so stubborn and proud that you refuse to obey the Holy Spirit. Instead you're busy trying to figure out how to destroy the men who bring the truth to you. You even killed the most important One of all, Jesus. Don't tell me about the Law, because you don't obey it yourselves."

"You can't talk to us like that!" shouted Annas. His face was beet red.

"Lies!" shouted Caiaphas.

"Lies about the Law! Lies about the temple!" angry voices chanted all round the room. "Lies about God!"

Stephen stood calmly in the council chamber as the leaders ranted and raved at him. Suddenly he could see beyond the chamber, because the Holy Spirit let him look right into Heaven.

"Look!" Stephen called out, pointing up at the ceiling. "I am seeing into Heaven, and there's Jesus standing at the right hand of God."

"We can't listen to these awful lies any longer!" Annas screamed, covering his ears.

"He doesn't deserve to live! Stone him! Stone him!" Voices all around agreed.

Like a mighty river, the men poured out of their seats and grabbed Stephen, sweeping him from the room. Through the city they stormed, dragging Stephen along. Angry, shouting people followed.

By the time they had reached the edge of the city, a mob boiled around the deacon. With angry shouts they picked up stones and began hurling them at Stephen. Looking toward Heaven, Stephen prayed, "Lord Jesus, let me come to You now."

And in a voice loud enough for the mob to hear,

Stephen shouted, "Lord, they don't know what they're doing, so don't hold my death against them." Then Stephen closed his eyes and died.

Annas dusted off his hands. "That's the end of that!" he said. He picked up his cloak and thanked young Saul who had been guarding the garments of the stoners.

Saul smiled, "Glad to help out." He watched as men carried Stephen's body away. "How could that man have been so peaceful?" Saul wondered. He shook his head trying to forget Stephen's face, and muttered, "These Jesus believers have gone too far. It's time that they were stopped."

Even as the believers were weeping over Stephen's body, Saul was getting permission from the council to arrest and punish other believers. He stormed wildly from house to house, dragging men and women off to prison and death.

"What should we do?" the believers asked one another. "There's no safe place for us in Jerusalem with this maniac Saul hunting us down day and night."

So many of the believers fled from the city and found safety in the outlying areas of Judea and Samaria. And wherever they traveled they spread the word about Jesus.

6. The Magician's Silver

The dusty road stretched out before Philip into the region called Samaria. He rested for a moment, looking back toward Jerusalem.

"I wonder how Peter and the others are holding up under Saul's attack," he thought. Like Stephen, Philip was a deacon and he had worked closely with the apostles. More and more believers were being thrown into prison, so the apostles had encouraged Philip to get out of Jerusalem while he could.

"I'd rather stay here and help you," Philip had protested.

Story based on Acts 8:5-25

"We'll be all right," John said. "We will be happier knowing that you are safely out of Jerusalem. Let us know where you are and how you are doing. Okay?" With his knapsack tied to his back, Philip left the city the next morning.

"Samaria is as good a place as any to live," the young man thought. Actually, this was a strange decision for Philip, who was a Jew.

Jews had hated Samaritans for hundreds of years, because long ago the Jews who lived in Samaria had married people who weren't Jews. That made them watered-down Jews, which was about the worst thing you could be.

Of course, Philip knew about the ancient feud, but he was filled with Jesus' love—even for the Samaritans. So he trudged ahead until he came to a Samaritan city. As soon as he arrived, he began telling everyone about Jesus.

After a few weeks, huge crowds were coming to hear Philip speak. One day, a magician named Simon decided to find out what the commotion was all about, so he traveled into the city to listen to Philip.

Simon was a good magician and he usually drew a fair-sized crowd when he performed his tricks. But here in the city he was amazed to see thousands of people all listening to Philip.

Simon squeezed between the people in the crowded square until he was close enough to see what was going on. He got there just in time to see Philip lay his hands on a crippled man. Suddenly the man jumped up and walked around—completely healed. Simon's mouth fell open. "How did Philip do that?" the magician wondered. "I'll have to get closer."

Simon pushed and shoved until he was at the front of the crowd. Philip was laying his hands on a woman who Simon knew was crazy. With a shout, an evil spirit left her body, and she smiled. She was well.

Everyone in the crowd cheered happily. They all believed in Jesus as the Son of God. Men and women were baptized that day, and there, in the midst of the new believers, was Simon.

Philip packed his knapsack once again and prepared to move on to the next town. Just as he was leaving the city, Simon the magician caught up with him.

"There's so much more I need to know about Jesus," Simon told Philip. "Please, let me travel with you. I won't cause any problems."

"Sure," Philip agreed. "It'll be nice having

someone to talk to on the road."

So in the early morning light, the two set off. They traveled together through several towns, and at each one Philip preached about the risen Savior. And he healed the sick people brought to him. And every time Philip performed a miracle, Simon wondered, "Now, how does he *do* that?"

Meanwhile, back in Jerusalem, the apostles began to hear about the work Philip was doing in Samaria. They also heard about the one big problem the church in Samaria had. There was no sign that the Holy Spirit had entered the new believers.

"Hmm," Peter thought while reading one of Philip's letters. "It sounds like Philip could use our help." Peter and John wasted no time, and a few days later the two apostles caught up with Philip and Simon.

"Round up the people you have baptized in the last few days," Peter requested.

Philip did. Then the apostles prayed that the Holy Spirit would come. John and Peter laid their hands on the heads of the believers. The Holy Spirit came into the believers with a surge of mighty power, and the believers all spoke in strange languages.

"These men from Jerusalem are powerful magicians," Simon thought. "This is the best spell I've ever seen."

Simon dug deeply into his knapsack and pulled out a bag of coins. He hurried back to the apostles and set the money on the table beside them.

"There are silver coins in the bag," he announced excitedly. "Please let me buy the power to bring the Holy Spirit to people when I lay my hands on them." Simon knew that powerful magic spells were expensive, and he was willing to pay John and Peter every coin he had.

Peter shoved the bag of coins back at Simon angrily. "You don't understand God at all if you think that your silver can buy His gift. You'd better ask God to forgive you because you're filled with jealousy and the desire to have power."

Simon's mouth dropped open in shock. At last he understood. The signs and miracles Philip and the apostles performed were not magic at all, but the power of God.

"What have I done?" he cried. "Please pray with me that I'll be forgiven."

7. Blinded by the Light!

As John and Peter approached Jerusalem, they met a family of believers heading north away from the city. After a happy greeting, the apostles asked, "How are things going in Jerusalem since we've been gone?"

The husband and wife looked at each other sadly over the heads of their children. The husband answered, "Terrible! That maniac Saul burst into our neighbor's home just a few nights ago, and hauled the man and his wife off to prison. They had only been believers for a few days." He put his arm around the youngest child.

Story based on Acts 9:1-19

"This little one is their son. We promised to take care of him."

"If something doesn't happen soon to stop Saul," the wife said, "there won't be one believer left in Jerusalem. Every day people leave to keep from being arrested. I hope we can return soon."

"Yes," Peter agreed. "We'll miss you." They said good-bye to the family, and a few hours later the apostles arrived in Jerusalem. They got there just in time to see Saul marching out of the city surrounded by official Jewish police.

"Where is he going?" John wondered, scratching his head. He stood aside for the little army to pass.

"I don't know," Peter shrugged. "But you can bet that believers are in for a rough time when he gets there. We'd better pray for them."

The apostles were right. Saul was up to no good. He heard how many believers had escaped from Jerusalem and had gone to live up north in Damascus. And he was determined to follow them, and arrest them there.

Saul was a very religious Jew, who spent much time studying the Scriptures and trying to carefully follow the laws of Moses. He honestly thought that he was doing God a favor by punishing the believers.

It was a long way to Damascus, and Saul had a lot of time to think as he marched along. He thought about his cruel acts against the church of Jesus, and Stephen's face kept popping into his mind.

"How could that man stay so calm as they stoned him?" thought Saul, bothered by the memory. "All he had to do to save his life was to admit that this Jesus thing is all a fake. I've got to stop thinking about him."

Step after step, Saul trudged on toward Damascus. Step after step, he was bothered by the memories of the joy and peace he had seen on the faces of believers who had been dragged off to prison. It just didn't make sense. How could so many people die believing a lie?

After marching for a week, the troop stopped to rest for a moment on the top of the hill overlooking Damascus. Saul looked down at the unsuspecting city and smiled. "If those Jesus followers think that they're safe from me here..." But before he could finish his thought, a brilliant light from heaven flashed in Saul's face, and surrounded him.

"Aagh!" Saul screamed, covering his eyes with his hands. But it was too late. The light had already burned his eyes, and it hurt so much that his knees buckled and he fell to the ground.

"Saul, why are you persecuting me?"

Saul, still digging his fists into his injured eyes, was confused. "Who are You, Lord?"

"I am Jesus," came the simple reply.

"Jesus!" thought Saul. He opened his eyes a crack to look, but the light hurt so much that he shut them again.

"I want you to get up," Jesus continued. "Go into Damascus. You'll meet someone there who will tell you what you are supposed to do." And the light disappeared.

"Master!" the guards huddled around Saul. "Are you all right?"

Saul, still rubbing his eyes, stumbled to his feet. "What did He look like?" he demanded.

"Look like? Who, Sir?" The puzzled guards looked at each other.

"Didn't you see a Man in the light? Didn't you hear Him speaking to me?"

"No, Sir," they answered. "We saw no man. But we did hear a voice. We thought you had been struck by lightning, because there was light all around for a minute."

Slowly, Saul opened his eyes, afraid of what he might see. But it was worse than he had imagined. He was completely blind!

*****

Three days later in Damascus, a Christian named Ananias was praying. "Ananias!" someone called out to him. Instantly he recognized the voice of his Master.

"I'm listening to You, Lord," he answered.

"I want you to find the house of a man named Judas on Straight Street. When you get there you'll find Saul, blind and praying. Lay your hands on him and he'll be able to see again."

"Saul in Damascus!" Ananias thought. "Lord," he said, "I've heard a lot of bad things about what Saul has done to the church in Jerusalem. Now that he's in Damascus, I'm sure he'll start arresting Christians here."

"Don't worry about that," Jesus replied. "Just go take care of him. I've chosen Saul to follow me and to go out into the world telling everyone the good news. But it won't be easy for him. Saul will suffer a lot because he follows me."

Ananias didn't stand around waiting to be told

a second time. He immediately started looking for Saul.

Saul had been at Judas' house for three days, and he was busy praying. He asked God to forgive him for hurting the church, and he asked Jesus to be his Savior.

"Brother Saul," Ananias greeted the man who had done so much to hurt Christians. "I've been sent by the Lord Jesus so that you might be able to see again."

Ananias gently laid his hands on Saul's head. Instantly, little scaly flakes dropped from Saul's eyes. He blinked a few times, and smiled.

"I can see!" he announced. "Now, Ananias, you must take me to be baptized."

8. Escape Through the Wall

Early the next morning, Saul hesitated outside a Jewish synagogue and whispered a quick prayer for courage. He knew that the Jews would think he had gone crazy. After all, he had come to arrest Christians, not join them.

Some of the Christians had advised Saul to start preaching in a city where no one knew him. But Saul realized that he had to start where his cruel past was known. He had to say to the Jews who had always respected him, "I was wrong. Look at the Scriptures and you, too, will discover that Jesus is the Messiah."

Story based on Acts 9:20-29

And that's exactly what he did.

"Jesus is the Son of God," he announced at every synagogue in Damascus. Saul knew the Scriptures like the back of his hand, and he showed the Jews verse after verse that proved his statement. They didn't all believe him, but he made such good sense that no one could argue against him.

Saul taught about Jesus in and around Damascus for three years, and he made a lot of enemies in the synagogues.

"Saul! Saul!" One of the Christians came running into the house where the preacher was staying. "The Jewish leaders are plotting to kill you."

"Slow down," Saul ordered. "Now tell me what this is all about."

"The leaders are worried that too many people are listening to you and believing," the messenger reported. "They're afraid of losing their power. Men are hiding near the city gate, hoping to catch you coming or going, so that no one will see them kill you."

"We've got to get you out of Damascus," Ananias said. "It isn't safe for you to be here any longer."

Late that night, a small group of Christians crept through the dark streets of Damascus with Saul. At every corner they hid, and looked up and down the deserted streets.

At last they reached the high city wall. They climbed a flight of steep steps to a house that was built right into the wall.

Tap! Tap! Tap! They softly knocked a secret code. The door creaked open, just wide enough for them to enter.

"Shush!" the woman warned them. "Don't wake the neighbors."

Ananias was already in the house. He stepped forward to greet Saul. "You'll have several hours of darkness to travel away from Damascus in safety," he told his friend. "Have you decided where you'll go now?"

"To Jerusalem," Saul answered. "It's time that the council hears about Jesus from me." He grinned and said good-bye to his friends. "Thanks for all of your help."

Ananias smiled at his Christian brother. "We'll miss you, Saul, but now it's time for you to go." Ananias led him to the window. Saul could see that it was a long drop to the ground below. He would land outside the city.

"Don't worry," Ananias chuckled. "We won't make you jump." He pointed to a large basket under the window with a heavy piece of rope tied to it. "Hop in."

With Saul crouched down in the basket, the men put it through the open window. They let it down, down into the dark night.

"The Lord go with you!" whispered the men and women.

Thud! Saul leaped out as the basket hit the ground, and he gave the rope a tug. Up it went, vanishing through the distant window. Saul stood alone outside the city for a few minutes. He thanked God for his good friends and for his successful escape.

But there was no time to lose. He crossed the fields, and then climbed up to the highway. He never looked back at Damascus, but headed eagerly for Jerusalem.

* * * * *

Several days later, Saul passed through the city gate of Jerusalem. He was really missing his Christian friends in Damascus.

"I can hardly wait to get together with the Christians in Jerusalem," he thought. "They'll be so shocked and happy that I'm now a follower of Jesus."

He was right about one thing. The Christians were shocked.

"Saul the Persecutor is back in town. Look out!" The word spread quickly. "He says he's a believer now, but that's probably just a sneaky way to find us. Don't trust him."

Saul could not find groups of Christians to talk to, because they were all hiding from him. All but one.

Saul heard a knock at the door of the house where he was staying, and opened it. There stood Joseph Barnabas, smiling.

"My old friend!" Barnabas greeted Saul, happily. "It's been so long since we've talked to each other. I've heard some exciting news about you—that you've become a Christian. Is that true?"

Saul invited Barnabas inside. "Yes, I met Jesus face to face on my way to Damascus three years ago." Then Saul told Barnabas all about the light, the voice, the blindness, and how he had narrowly escaped death at the hands of the Jewish leaders.

"It sounds like you really are one of us now." Barnabas laughed.

"I can hardly wait to talk to Christians here in Jerusalem. But everyone is hiding from me," Saul said sadly.

"Be patient," Barnabas told him. "You were pretty rough on us once, and everyone is still afraid of you. But I think I can help. Come on, let's go see Peter."

Barnabas introduced Saul to Peter, and Saul explained what had happened to him. After that the church opened up to the new apostle. He was happy to have Christian friends again.

And of course, he had a lot to tell everyone he met including the men he had known in the government. Now, the Christians rejoiced at having Saul in Jerusalem, but the leaders were furious with him—quite a turnaround.

9. A Message in a Bundle

It was just about lunchtime when Peter stood up and stretched his legs.

"I'm glad you could stay with us for a few days here in Joppa," said Simon the Tanner. He gave Peter a friendly slap on the back.

"You know we don't get to Jerusalem very often," Simon's neighbor agreed. "And we love to hear about Jesus. So your visit has been special."

"I enjoy coming here," Peter said. "And it's not just for the good fellowship. I love the sea. It reminds me of the days when I fished for a living

Story based on Acts 10:1-23

and of the first time I met Jesus."

Simon nodded. "I know what you mean. Would you like to spend a little time by yourself while my wife fixes our noon meal?"

"Yes," Peter admitted, anxious to get out into the fresh sea air. "I'd like to pray."

Simon directed the apostle up the stairs that led to the house's flat roof. "It's cool up here," he told Peter. "And no one will bother you."

Simon's house was right on the beach of the Mediterranean Sea. And from the roof, Peter could look out across the blue water. The bright sun sparkled on the waves. "Cool and quiet," thought Peter as he knelt to pray.

As Peter prayed, God sent him a vision. He saw something gigantic being lowered right out of Heaven.

As it came nearer, he could see that it was a huge sheet joined at the corners. It looked like a huge picnic bundle. The bundle was so close for a moment that Peter could look into it. It was filled with all kinds of birds and animals.

"Take your pick, Peter," a Voice called out. "Kill it and eat."

Peter was amazed by this unusual command. Jewish people had strict rules about which animals they could eat and which ones they couldn't. Everyone who wasn't Jewish was called Gentile, and the Gentiles weren't particular about what they ate. The Jews, however, were proud of their eating laws, and they looked down their noses at the Gentiles who would eat anything. Now this voice from Heaven was telling Peter to pick *any* kind of meat.

"I can't do that," Peter called back. "I've never eaten anything that was against our laws."

The Voice boomed again. "You shouldn't put down anything that God says is all right." And the bundle came toward him a second time. "Kill and eat, Peter." The sheet lifted and returned again.

The apostle stared at the animals and birds in the bundle, and heard the voice offer him food for a third time. "God is telling you that this meat is all right for you."

As the bundle vanished into Heaven for the third time, the Holy Spirit spoke to Peter. "Three men are looking for you. Go with them and don't worry, because I'm the one who sent them."

Peter didn't have much time to think about the vision, because just then there was a knock at the door. Simon called up to the apostle, "You've got company!"

Peter hurried to the door, and to his surprise, he was greeted by a Roman soldier and two Roman servants—Gentiles.

"We are here to take you to my commander, Cornelius, in the city of Caesarea," the soldier explained. "Will you come?"

The next morning, Peter and some of his friends headed toward Caesarea with the three Romans.

10. Something Missing Is Found

Cornelius sighed heavily. He had everything that a man could want, but something seemed to be missing.

"Why am I not happy?" he wondered. "I like my job. I'm a centurion in the Roman army, and the commander of a company of soldiers. I'm proud to be in charge.

"And I have a nice family." He smiled, thinking of his wife and kids. "I'm lucky to have them here with me in Caesarea.

"I even like being stationed in the country of Palestine," he admitted. "It's a hot, dusty place.

Story based on Acts 10:24-48

And the people here don't like Romans very much. But if I hadn't come here I might never have found out about God." Cornelius sighed again.

Romans believed that there were hundreds of gods—one for the ocean, one for the sun, one for trees, and on and on. Cornelius had learned that the Jews believed in only one God who had created the universe and who watched over them day after day. So he had asked the Jewish teachers lots of questions.

Cornelius, along with his family and servants, had turned his back on the Roman religion and had believed in the powerful God of the Jews. He now served God joyfully, praying often and giving freely to the poor.

But now Cornelius knew that simply believing in God wasn't enough to make him happy. There was something else he had to do.

He loved God with all his heart. So one afternoon he knelt and prayed, "Lord God, You have filled my life, but now I think there's something missing. Show me what it is."

"Cornelius," a voice called to him. The centurion turned quickly, and what he saw scared the wits out of him. An angel of God stood in the room.

With his knees shaking, Cornelius answered, "What do you want with me?"

"I was sent to tell you that your prayers and your giving to the poor haven't been ignored by God. Send men to the city of Joppa to find Peter. He's staying with Simon the Tanner near the sea."

Cornelius wondered, "Who is Peter, and why should I send for him?" But the centurion decided that he should obey the angel without asking too many questions. He called for a soldier who believed in God, and two of his servants, and commanded them to go to Joppa and bring Peter back to Caesarea.

* * * * *

Cornelius paced excitedly back and forth across the tile floor. It had been four days since his men had left for Joppa, and he knew that Peter would be arriving soon. He had invited his relatives and several friends to meet Peter and hear what he had to tell them about God.

The soldier escorted Peter into the room where Cornelius was waiting. As soon as the centurion saw him, he fell down at the apostle's feet saying, "My lord!"

"You don't have to bow before me," Peter said, gently helping the centurion stand up. "I'm just a man, like you."

Cornelius led Peter into his home and introduced him to his family and friends. Peter was amazed to find so many Gentiles gathered to hear him.

"You all know about Jews," Peter began. "So you know it is against our laws for me to even come into this house of Gentiles. But God showed me something the other day." Peter recalled the voice assuring him that he should accept whatever God says is right, and now he understood what the bundle had meant.

"You and I are all people before God. If God accepts you, then I accept you, too. Tell me why you wanted me to come here."

"An angel told me to send for you," Cornelius explained. "You must have something to tell us about God."

"God accepts you all because you love Him and want to do what's right," Peter said. "I've been sent to tell you about Jesus, the Son of God." So Peter told the Gentiles how Jesus had lived and died, and they all listened carefully.

"We apostles walked and talked with Jesus after He rose up from death. And He commanded us to tell everyone about Him, and that He will be the

One who judges the living and the dead.

"The prophets told us that Jesus would come to save us from the judgment of death. All you have to do is believe in Him, and He will forgive you for the sins that have separated you from God."

As Peter spoke, the Holy Spirit burst into the room and filled everyone. The Jewish believers who had come with Peter were surprised, because the Gentiles began speaking other languages. The Holy Spirit had come to people who were not Jews.

Peter was thrilled to be a brother in Christ with these Romans. He asked the Jewish believers, "Is there anyone here who doesn't think these new Christians should be baptized? After all, they've received the Holy Spirit of God." No one disagreed.

After the baptism, Peter stayed with Cornelius for several days, teaching him more about Jesus. And the centurion knew that at last the empty spot in his life had been filled by the Lord.

11. Break Out!

Before too long, the word got around that Peter had preached the good news about Jesus to Gentiles. The Jewish leaders were wickedly delighted.

"Breaking the Law again," they whispered one to another. "No one will want to protect Peter when they hear that he's talking to Gentiles now."

The apostles had been safe in Jerusalem for years, because everyone respected them for their courage. But now that they were openly friendly to Gentiles, the apostles lost their popularity and their safety.

Story based on Acts 12:1-24

The Romans were the ones who really controlled the country. So Herod, the Jewish king, was always looking for something to do.

When it came to his attention that the apostles were breaking laws concerning Gentiles, Herod assembled his advisers. He said, "I think the people are getting tired of these Jesus preachers." Herod went on, "I'm going to have one of the leaders arrested to see how the people react. Who should it be?"

The pleased advisers were happy to make a suggestion. "How about arresting James, the brother of John? He was one of Jesus' disciples, and he's been a bother to us lately."

Herod sent the guards out immediately to bring back James. "What will you do with him?" the advisors asked.

"Put him on trial," Herod answered, "and sentence him to death. That's the best way to test public opinion."

When James was brought before Herod, the king pronounced him guilty. "Kill him," he calmly ordered the guards.

"Have you heard?" people exclaimed everywhere. "Herod has killed one of those Jesus preachers."

"Good riddance," many people agreed. "Maybe Herod will have them all killed and we won't have to listen to them bellyache about *our* sins anymore."

Herod was so pleased with the results of his experiment that he sent out guards to arrest a more active apostle. This time they threw Peter into prison.

"This man is tricky. Don't let him escape," Herod warned the commander of the prison guards. "Watch him day and night."

The commander decided not to take any chances, so he assigned four guards on each shift. And he chained Peter to two of the guards.

* * * * *

Peter looked at the heavy chains on his arms. He had been sitting on the cold stone floor between the guards for nearly a week now.

"At least I won't have to stay in prison forever," he thought. He knew that in the morning he would be judged by Herod.

But Peter wasn't afraid. He knew that God had everything under control, so Peter fell asleep peacefully. But all over Jerusalem, believers were awake, praying for their brother Peter.

Suddenly Peter was jolted awake by a sharp jab in

his side. The prison cell was flooded with light.

"I must be dreaming," Peter thought.

Hands tugged at his shoulders. "Get up, Peter, and get dressed!" a voice whispered urgently.

"Huh?" Peter blinked his eyes. In the light he saw the silhouette of a person standing before him. He rubbed his sleepy eyes. "My hands! They're free!" The chains lay in a pile between the sleeping guards. "Now I *know* I'm dreaming!"

"Follow me quickly," said the man in the light as he motioned to Peter. Peter pulled on his sandals and gathered his cloak around him. The two walked out of the prison cell, past the guards.

"Stay close to me," the man told Peter, and again they passed the guards as if they were invisible. Peter was beginning to wonder what the dream meant, when he saw the iron gate of the prison swing open. The air outside was fresh and cool, and Peter took a deep breath. "Can you tell me the meaning of this dream?" He turned to the man, but the street was dark and empty. Peter was alone.

Peter glanced over his shoulder to make sure he wasn't being followed. Then he turned into the dark alley that led to John Mark's house. When he reached the door, he knocked softly.

"Who's there?" a tiny voice asked. Peter knew this was the maid, Rhoda. She was also a Christian.

"Rhoda," he whispered back, "it's me, Peter." He heard her squeal happily. But instead of letting him into the house, she turned around and hurried back inside.

"Mistress! Mistress!" Rhoda ran into the large room where many Christians were gathered, praying for Peter.

"Calm down, girl," said Mary, John Mark's mother. "Who was at the door so late?"

"Peter!" Rhoda shouted to the whole group. "Peter is well, and he's standing at the door."

"Poor girl," said John Mark. He took Rhoda's hand. "You're just tired from being up all night."

"No!" she cried. "He really is at the door!"

"Maybe you've seen his angel," Mary suggested. "Sit down, Rhoda. We need to start praying again."

Meanwhile, out on the doorstep, Peter was getting tired of waiting. He knocked again, very softly. No answer. So, he knocked again, softly. Still no answer. Peter took a deep breath and pounded the door loudly three times.

"Someone is still knocking," Mary said. And she

went to the door herself with several others.

"Peter!" they all exclaimed when the door was opened. "What are you doing here? You're supposed to be in prison." Everyone was talking at once.

"Shhh!" Peter hissed. "Let's go inside and talk. We might wake up the neighbors out here, and I'm in no hurry to go back to prison."

They all gathered inside, and Peter told them about his escape. "I will have to hide for awhile," he said. "Let everyone know that God answered your prayers."

Before daybreak, Peter said good-bye to his friends, and crept out into the streets of Jerusalem. He didn't tell anyone where he was going.

By the time the sun rose, Peter was long gone. In prison, the guards who had been chained to Peter woke up and gasped with horror.

"He's gone!" they yelled. "Why did you let him out of the cell?" They angrily accused the soldiers who had guarded the door all night.

"We didn't let him out!" the soldiers argued. "Why did you release him from the chains?"

"We didn't! He just . . . disappeared!"

Of course they searched for the missing prisoner high and low. And when Herod heard that Peter was gone, he blew up.

"I warned you!" he bellowed at the commander. "Take those four guards out and kill them!"

Herod stayed angry for quite awhile, but he didn't live long enough to find Peter. One day, Herod dressed in shining silver. He came out before the people and sat on his throne. Everyone wanted to please him, so they said, "You are more like a god than a man."

Herod smiled and thought, "They're right. I am like God." But Someone didn't agree with Herod, and that Someone was God Himself.

Immediately, Herod fell down with a terrible illness, and soon he died.

Peter was safe from Herod, and so was the church. No one, not even a king, could stand in the way of God's Word. And the church in Judea kept right on growing.

But it was time to spread the word about Jesus beyond Judea. And the church knew just who to send on that dangerous mission.

12. The First Missionaries

Paul and Barnabas were on their way to Galatia. On the first part of their long journey, they sailed from Antoich to the island of Cyprus.

There they met the Roman governor. They told him and many others about Jesus. And it was probably on the island that Saul's name was changed to Paul.

After teaching on the island for awhile, Paul and Barnabas sailed on to the coast of Asia Minor. They didn't stay on the coast for long. They hiked up the perilous road into the mountains. The people in Pamphylia had warned them that

Story based on Acts 13:1—14:20

bandits lurked along the lonely road. And if the bandits didn't get them, there was always the chance of being eaten by a bear or a lion.

But Paul and Barnabas were determined to cross the mountains. After all, no one had promised them that being missionaries would be easy.

"Do you think we'll make it to Pisidian Antioch by nightfall?" Barnabas asked Paul. "It would be nice to sleep under a roof tonight."

"I agree," Paul answered. He shifted his small pack of food and clothing. "Maybe we'll meet some travelers who can tell us how far we have to go." They trudged on up the rugged road that was sometimes no more than a path across fallen rocks.

"Let me carry your pack for a while," Barnabas offered. Paul had been sick while they were on the coast. He wasn't fully recovered yet, but he had insisted on making the journey. Gratefully, Paul slipped off the pack and handed it to his old friend.

"I'm sure I'll feel better when we reach Pisidian Antioch," Paul said, stretching his sore back.

The travelers met no one all day. But just as they were thinking of setting up camp for the night, they reached the pass. There below them was the town. Cheerfully, they walked the last few miles into Antioch and found an inn. After washing off the road dirt, the two men enjoyed a peaceful night under a real roof.

In the morning they went right to work. They found the town's synagogue where the local Jews worshiped.

"We must always take the good news to the Jews first," Paul advised. "And then we'll go to the Gentiles. That's how Jesus wants us to spread His message."

Paul and Barnabas walked into the synagogue and sat down. The Jews there were delighted to see visitors.

"Do you have anything you'd like to share with us?" they asked the missionaries.

Paul didn't have to be asked twice. He stood and began to tell about the prophets and the great men of the old Scriptures. Everyone listened.

"God has made the old prophecies come true," Paul announced. "We've come to tell you about the One called Jesus whom God raised from death. Jesus never sinned, but was perfect in every way. Through Him God forgives us for our sins."

The worshipers rejoiced. "That's the news we've been waiting for all of our lives. Please come back next week so other people can hear about Jesus."

The following week the synagogue was packed. Almost everyone in town came to hear how to be forgiven of their sins. But not all the people received the missionaries' news joyfully.

"We're in danger of losing our powerful positions to these men from Judea," the leaders moaned to each other. "We've got to get rid of them before too many people believe what they are teaching."

The leaders stirred up a mob and kicked Paul and Barnabas out of town. But that didn't bother the missionaries. They just headed for the next village.

In each town that Paul and Barnabas visited, some people believed their message about Jesus. And some people tried to hurt and even kill them.

In the town of Lystra, some of the angry people from Pisidian Antioch caught up with Paul and Barnabas.

"That's him!" they shouted wildly to the crowd that was gathered listening to Paul. "He's the one who lies about God." The mob boiled around Paul, throwing him to the ground.

"Kill him!" someone cried out. "Stone him!"

Rocks hurtled through the air and struck Paul's face and body. He covered his head with his bleeding hands and fell over, unconscious. Men from the mob gathered around the still body. One man even nudged Paul with his foot.

"He's dead!" they cheered, satisfied that they had accomplished their job. "Quick! Throw the body outside the town so we can't be blamed for his death." Rough hands grabbed Paul's shoulders and legs, and dumped him in a ditch a little way from town.

The Chrisitans followed behind so that they could give Paul a decent funeral. But when they found his muddy, blood-stained body, they were surprised to see it move.

"He's alive! Hurry! Get him out of the ditch!" they all shouted. And they helped Paul climb up to the road. He hobbled painfully back to town and found Barnabas. The next morning, they traveled on.

Everywhere they went, many men and women believed in Jesus and were saved. It wasn't an easy journey, but the new Christians were glad that Paul and Barnabas had the courage and faith in God to make it.

13. Earthquake in Philippi

Paul breathed in the fresh salty air. It was good to be traveling again. His first journey with Barnabas had been successful. And now he was in the midst of his second journey, this time with a man named Silas. They had visited many of the new churches. Young Timothy had joined them, and also a Gentile doctor named Luke.

Paul stood at the bow of the sailing boat, and watched as the busy harbor at Neapolis came into view. "New cities filled with people who have never heard about Jesus," Paul thought. He was eager to land and start teaching.

Story based on Acts 16:1-40

When the boat reached shore, he was the first one out. "Hurry up!" he urged Silas and Luke. "We still have a long walk ahead of us." They slung their packs on their backs and headed toward the bustling city of Philippi.

Philippi was a Roman colony, and a major city on the trade route. When the travelers entered the city, they were immediately surrounded by merchants.

"Wouldn't you like to buy a lovely bracelet for your wife? I'll sell it to you cheaper than any jeweler in the marketplace."

"I'll tell your fortune for a few pennies," a young slave girl begged the missionaries.

"No thanks," Paul kindly refused both offers.

"Look at all of this fresh fruit!" Luke exclaimed. "How much for a pomegranate?"

"Twenty-five cents," the merchant replied.

"Too much." Luke reluctantly put the fruit back.

"For you, fifteen cents." The merchant held out the fruit.

"All right," Luke agreed, taking the ripe pomegranate. The missionaries pushed through the crowded marketplace. Everywhere they went in Philippi, people were busy making money—or spending it.

There was no synagogue in Philippi. When the Jewish day of worship came, Paul asked around and learned that Jewish women met at a quiet place by the riverside.

Paul, Silas, Luke and Timothy went down to the river. "There they are," Silas said, pointing to a small group of women who were worshiping.

"Hello there," Paul called to them. "Don't be afraid. Silas and I are Jews from Judea. We're here to tell you some good news about the Messiah." The women listened, and many of them believed and were baptized right then and there.

The following week Paul and his companions headed to the river again to pray and teach. The young slave girl ran along beside them.

"Isn't that the girl who tells fortunes in the marketplace?" Silas asked. "Her owners sure make a lot of money with her. It seems like everyone here wants to know his fortune."

"I'm sure there is an evil spirit living in her," Paul said seriously, watching the girl dance around them.

Suddenly she let out a hair-raising shriek. Everyone on the street turned to see what had happened. She called out loudly, "These men are followers of the one God, and they're here to tell you how to be saved."

If she had only done this once, the missionaries probably would have ignored it. But day after day, she ran up to them and started screaming out her message.

Paul was getting tired of the fortune-teller. So he finally grabbed her and commanded, "Evil spirit within this girl, leave her now in the name of Jesus Christ." Since a spirit must obey Jesus, it fled from the girl's body instantly. She no longer had the power to tell fortunes, but she was free from the evil spirit.

"Look what those men have done to your fortune-teller," a merchant teased the girl's owners. "You won't be making money with her anymore."

"Why didn't you mind your own business and leave our girl alone?" the slave's owners shouted angrily to Paul. "You've ruined us! You're going to pay!" The crowd agreed and swarmed around Paul and Silas and dragged them to the judges.

"These Jews are disturbing our city's peace," the slave's owners complained. "They're teaching the people ideas that aren't Roman."

"Punish them for bothering us!" the crowd cheered.

"Gladly!" the judges shouted. "Guards, take these men out and beat them. Then throw them into prison."

Paul and Silas were whipped until their backs were raw and bleeding. Then they were hauled off to jail.

"These men are criminals against Rome," the guards told the jailer. "Don't let them escape or you'll be sorry."

"I'll take care of them," the jailer said. He knew that the guards meant business. He shut Paul and Silas in a cell that was deep within the prison, and locked their legs in heavy wooden stocks.

You'd think that Paul and Silas would be miserable with sore backs and aching legs locked in stocks. But they were too busy praying and singing hymns to worry about how they felt. The other prisoners were listening to them, too. It was just about midnight when the ground began to rumble softly, then a little louder, and then— BOOM! A gigantic earthquake ripped through the prison like an explosion and broke open the doors, chains, and even the stocks.

The jailer had been snoozing at the prison gate. When the earthquake struck it knocked him off his stool. He shook his head in amazement and cried out, "Oh, no! The cells are open. Everyone has escaped. The judges will have me beaten to death." The jailer drew his sword and was just about ready to kill himself, when someone yelled, "Stop!"

It was Paul. "Don't kill yourself. No one has escaped. Come on in and see for yourself."

The jailer looked inside the cell, and saw that all the prisoners were indeed still there. He was so impressed that the Jews cared enough about him not to escape that he fell down before them and asked, "How can I be saved?"

"Believe that Jesus is God's Son, and you will be saved," Paul told the jailer. Immediately the jailer believed. He took Paul and Silas to his house to care for their wounds and give them food. Everyone in his family listened to the message that Paul had brought to Philippi. All of them believed and were baptized that same night.

Paul and Silas may have returned to the prison cell before daybreak so the jailer wouldn't be in trouble for letting them go. At ant rate, in the morning they were officially released.

A few hours later, with their packs on their backs, the missionaries were on the road again.

14. Paul Imprisoned

The ship to Caesarea was ready to sail. The believers from Tyre gathered around Paul on the sandy beach. "We wish you wouldn't go to Jerusalem. There's danger waiting for you there."

"I've been in danger more than once," Paul said grimly, recalling the mobs and prisons and beatings he had faced for more than twenty years. "God is always beside me, looking after me," he assured them.

"It's time for us to board the ship," Luke said. Everyone kneeled down on the warm sand and prayed for the safety of the missionaries. Then Paul

Story based on Acts 21:1—23:24

and Luke waded out to the rowboat that carried them to the ship.

After climbing on board, the two travelers waved to the little crowd still standing near the shore. As the great square sail was hoisted, the wind caught it with a jolt. Paul and Luke were on their way again, this time heading for Jerusalem.

This was the last part of their long, third journey to start new churches and visit the older ones. Paul was anxious to report to the apostles how well the churches were doing in the Gentile countries.

When the ship landed at Caesarea, Paul and Luke hurried to Philip's house. Philip was still as busy as ever sharing the message about Jesus with everyone he met.

"Welcome home." He greeted the travelers happily. "It's been years since we've seen each other. Tell me about your journey." The three men settled down for a good visit.

After the missionaries had been in Caesarea for several days, a prophet from Judea came to see them with an urgent message. His name was Agabus.

"Give me your belt," he ordered Paul. Agabus tied up his own hands and feet with Paul's belt. Then he said, "The Holy Spirit says that whoever owns this belt will be tied up by the Jews in Jerusalem, and handed over to the Gentiles."

"That's the second warning!" Luke exclaimed. "You can't go to Jerusalem now, Paul."

"Stay here," begged the believers who had met Paul at Philip's house.

"I appreciate your concern," Paul replied, "but I feel I must go, even if I end up in prison. Please don't try to change my mind. Just pray that I will do what God wants me to do."

Paul and Luke packed their knapsacks and started the trek to Jerusalem.

* * * * *

"It's great to have you back with us," James and the apostles told Paul and Luke when they arrived in Jerusalem.

"I have so much to tell you about what God is doing among the Gentiles," Paul said as they gathered around to hear about the new churches.

When Paul finished, the apostles praised God. They then encouraged Paul to worship in the temple to show the Jews that he still respected Jewish laws. But the plan backfired.

Jews from the distant countries where Paul had preached about Jesus saw him in the temple.

"That's the man who wants everyone to stop following the Law," they shouted angrily. "He even brought Gentiles into the temple." That really stirred up the people, even though it was a lie. And they dragged Paul out of the temple in a rage.

"Come quickly," a Roman soldier told his commander. "The Jews have gone crazy. They're trying to kill someone in the middle of a riot."

The worst thing that a Roman commander could do was to lose control of the people he ruled. He could be put to death for allowing a riot. So the commander didn't waste any time sending soldiers into the mob to save Paul.

The crowd swarmed around the soldiers, tearing and leaping at the apostle. The people shouted wildly, "Kill him! Kill him!" No matter which way they turned, the angry people fought to rip Paul away from the guards. Finally, the soldiers lifted Paul over their heads and carried him above the mob to safety.

Paul was safe, but he wasn't free. The commander held Paul in the Roman headquarters until they could decide what to do with him.

One night, Jesus appeared to Paul in his room. He said, "Be brave, Paul, because I want you to go to Rome to tell about me." And Jesus was gone as quietly and quickly as He had appeared.

* * * * *

"Uncle Paul," called Paul's nephew, rushing into the Roman headquarters. "A group of men took a vow today that they won't eat or drink until they kill you."

"How many men are in on this plan?" Paul asked the young man.

"More than forty," he answered breathlessly. "What can we do?"

"Centurion," Paul called to one of the guards. "Take my nephew to see the commander. He's got important news."

"The Jews are plotting to kill my uncle," the nephew told the commander. "They plan to ask you to let Paul come to the council so they can question him. But on the way, a large group of men will ambush and kill him."

"Go home and don't worry," the commander said. "And don't tell anyone what you've told me. All right?"

Late that night, a small army galloped out of Jerusalem headed for the Roman governor's stronghold in Caesarea. In the midst of the army rode Paul.

15. Shipwreck!

"At last!" Paul thought. "I'm headed for Rome." For two long years, Paul stayed cooped up in the governor's palace in Caesarea. His friends were free to visit him, and he wasn't forced to stay in a dark cell, but it had still been prison.

A new governor came to rule in Caesarea, and the Jewish leaders asked him to let them judge Paul. But the apostle refused to be dragged back to Jerusalem.

"I haven't done anything wrong," Paul protested. "If I am tried by anyone, let it be Caesar himself." And the new governor gave the apostle

Story based on Acts 27:1-44

permission to take his case to Rome.

Now Paul stood on the deck of a ship watching Judea disappear beyond the eastern horizon. He would never see this land again, but that didn't stop him from being excited.

"Master?" Aristarchus broke into Paul's thoughts. "Our baggage is all stored for the voyage. Can I do anything else for you?"

Paul smiled at his old friend from Thessalonica. Aristarchus had willingly become Paul's slave so that he could travel with the prisoner to Rome.

"No, thanks," Paul answered. "You've done enough for now. Where's Luke?"

"Helping out with a seasick passenger," Aristarchus replied. Paul nodded, happy that both Luke and Aristarchus were with him on this final journey.

Paul and the other prisoners wandered around the ship. But the centurion, Julius, and his soldiers were never out of sight. If any of the prisoners were to jump overboard and escape, Julius knew that he would be in a lot of trouble. But the centurion didn't worry about Paul escaping, because he knew that the apostle could hardly wait to get to Rome.

After several days at sea, the ship landed in the

port of Myra. Julius scouted the harbor and found a large grain ship that was bound for Italy. The soldiers marched the prisoners on board.

The great square sail was hoisted up the tall mast in the center of the deck. The ship slipped gracefully out of the harbor toward the open sea.

The going was not easy. A sharp head wind battered the ship day and night, just about blowing it backwards. Finally the wind grew so strong that the captain decided to sail south with it. The ship anchored by the island of Crete at Fair Havens.

"We could be in a lot of danger if we try to sail any farther this late in the year," Paul warned the captain and Julius. "You could lose all of your cargo, not to mention your ship and the lives of all the people who are on board."

"You don't know what you're talking about," snapped the captain. "You're just a prisoner, and I sail across here every year. It's still safe to sail along the coast of Crete until we get to Phoenix. There's a better harbor there where we can wait for spring."

So the grain ship left Fair Havens. But the good weather didn't last long.

Paul watched the sky and saw the dark stormy

clouds begin to build. Suddenly, the wind changed direction, and a cold blast from the north rocked the ship violently.

The howling wind beat at the sail. Since the ship couldn't sail into the wind, the captain decided to let the wind have its way. With a mighty groan, the ship turned and raced south with the wind blasting it out toward the open sea.

The storm broke with full fury. Giant waves crashed across the deck and beat at the hull. The mast creaked with the strain of the gale and the ship rode the waves like a roller coaster out of control.

"Tie up the ship," the captain shouted over the ear-piercing scream of the wind. The sailors tugged on great leather straps that circled the hull of the ship, and tied them up tightly, hoping to keep the ship in one piece.

The next morning dawned with furious black clouds hiding the sun. And the ship was still battered by the wind, the waves and the rain.

"We're too low in the water," the captain called again. "We'll sink if we don't throw some cargo overboard." So the sailors heaved sacks of wheat into the swirling water. But that still wasn't enough.

"Throw out all of the spare equipment," commanded the captain, and the angry sea swallowed ropes and chains and oars. But even that wasn't enough, and everyone on the ship gave up hope of living through the terrible storm.

Everyone, that is, except Paul. And he had a good reason for not being afraid. As he prayed, he listened to the storm tearing the ship apart. He opened his eyes, and there beside him stood a shining angel.

"Don't be afraid, Paul," the angel said. "God wants you to speak to Caesar. You will live through the storm, and so will everyone who sails with you."

Paul scrambled onto the deck and called out to the men, "You didn't listen to me when you should have back at Fair Havens, but at least hear me now. The ship is going to be wrecked, but no one will die. God's angel told me, and I believe God."

The ship drifted for two weeks in the stormy sea. Late one night the sailors heard a frightening sound—waves crashing on rocks.

'We're going to run into the rocky shore," they whispered nervously. They stared into the dark night, but they couldn't see a thing. They measured the depth of the water, and to their horror, they discovered that the sea was getting more and more shallow.

"I wish morning would come," one said.

"Let's get out of here now," another sailor whispered. "We can take the lifeboat and get safely to shore."

Paul saw the sailors lowering the small boat, and he rushed to find Julius. "These men must stay on the ship or you and your soldiers will die."

Julius wasn't about to doubt Paul anymore. "Stop those sailors," he ordered his men. The soldiers ran to the side of the ship, and shoved the sailors away from the lifeboat. "We all stay on the ship," Julius told the sailors sharply. "Cut the lifeboat's ropes," he ordered. And the lifeboat was swept away, disappearing into the dark night.

As the sky began to grow light, Paul looked around at the frightened, hopeless faces of the sailors and soldiers. No one had eaten for days.

"Come on, everyone." Paul encouraged them. "Let's all eat and get some strength back. No one is going to die." Paul took a loaf of bread, and after thanking God for it, he ate.

"He must know what he's talking about," the men whispered. "Look how calm he is. Come on, let's eat, too."

* * * * *

As the morning sun slowly rose, the men on the ship began to make out the rocky shore. Thunder still growled in the stormy sky, and the sea waves still boiled angrily around the groaning ship.

"Can you tell where we are?" Julius asked the captain.

He shook his head, studying the coastline. "No, I've never been here before. But look over there." He pointed to a little bay with a sandy beach. "Maybe we can sail the ship safely to shore there."

"It's worth a try," Julius agreed.

"Cast off the anchors," the captain ordered, and the sailors cut the anchors loose. "Hoist the sail to the wind," he commanded again.

The sail was lifted on the mast. The wind filled it with a sharp jolt, and the ship began to pick up speed, heading directly for the beach.

"Oh, no!" the captain shouted. What he saw struck fear in his heart. A sandbar just below the water's surface blocked the ship's course to the beach.

The sailors screamed, rushing to take the sail down, but it was too late. The ship was racing across the water. No one could stop it now.

The ship struck the sandbar with a sickening crunch, and the men were knocked around the deck. The stormy surf pounded the ship's deck and smashed against the cracked hull.

"She's breaking up. The surf is crushing the ship." Everyone screamed as panic swept through the crew and passengers.

"Don't let the prisoners escape," the soldiers cried out. "Kill them!"

"No," ordered Julius, making sure that Paul would be kept alive. "Don't worry about the prisoners. Everyone who can swim, go on now and get to shore. Everyone else, grab onto something that will float."

It wasn't long before the ship broke apart on the sandbar. Sailors and soldiers and passengers struggled through the wild surf toward the beach.

One by one, the tired men washed up onto the shore and just as Paul had been promised, not one of them drowned.

16. Rome At Last

The men from the shipwreck huddled together on the beach. The rainy wind swirled around their wet bodies, chilling them to the bone. But before long, a group of people who lived on the island ran out to the beach to greet the marooned travelers.

"We saw your ship crash and break apart," they called out excitedly. "Did you all make it safely to shore?"

"No one drowned," Julius answered, "but if we don't dry off soon and get warm, we may all freeze to death." So they all set about the task of building

Story based on Acts 28:1-31

a huge bonfire.

Paul shuffled through the sand carrying an armful of driftwood and sticks. As he dumped the wood on the blazing fire, a snake wriggled out of the sticks and sank its fangs into his hand.

The island people screamed and pointed at Paul. "He'll die from that bite. He must be a murderer. He escaped dying in the sea, but now justice will kill him with the snake."

Paul felt the sting of the bite and saw the snake hanging from his hand. But without flinching, he shook his arm sharply. The snake lost its grip and flew with a sizzle into the crackling hot fire. Then Paul went about his work as if nothing had happened.

The islanders stared at him all day. "Just wait," they told each other. "Pretty soon his hand will swell up and he'll drop dead." But Paul kept walking around. He hardly took time to rest.

"He's not even getting sick," the islanders whispered. "He must have special powers."

As evening came, a man named Publius, who owned that part of the island, offered to let the shipwrecked men stay with him for a few days. Paul found out that Publius' father was sick with a terrible disease, so the apostle went to visit him.

Paul laid his hands on the sick man and prayed, "Dear Lord, in the name of Jesus, make this man well." And instantly, Publius' father felt better and got out of bed.

People all over the island heard about this. They flocked to Paul to receive healing for all kinds of illnesses. And the people were so grateful, that they showered the missionaries with gifts. They stocked their ship full of supplies for the last part of the trip to Italy.

* * * * *

After the winter had passed, a ship with Paul and his guards and companions on board sailed from the island. They had a calm voyage. The ship beached at the harbor of Puteoli. A group of Christians who lived in that town invited Paul and his friends to stay with them before heading overland to Rome. Paul was delighted to find that word about Jesus had spread so far.

A week later, Julius assembled the company of soldiers and prisoners and started the march to Rome.

The highway to Rome was wide and busy. Large carts carried merchandise to Rome from the harbor city. Companies of Roman soldiers patrolled the road, guarding the travelers from bandits and other dangers.

Paul thought about all of the lonely, faraway places he had traveled. He had taken God's Word across mountain passes and through stormy seas. And now, with each step, he was carrying the message of God's love for all mankind closer and closer to the mighty capital of the world—Rome. How would the proud citizens of Rome accept the message? Would they listen and believe, or would they sentence Paul to death?

When the company of soldiers and prisoners reached the town called Three Taverns, several miles from Rome, Paul's prayer was answered.

"That's him," a group of joyful people cheered, rushing up to Paul and his friends. "Hello, Brother Paul. Welcome to Rome!"

"We're happy to have you with us at last." The leader of the group stepped forward and hugged Paul. "We are Christians from Rome, the ones you wrote a letter to. We couldn't wait for you to arrive, so we hiked up here to meet you."

Paul grinned from ear to ear. "I thank God for all of you!" he exclaimed. "You'll never know how wonderful it is to know that there are believers everywhere—even in Rome." They sang happy songs about the Lord and praised God all the way into the city.

* * * * *

Paul remained a prisoner in Rome for the next two years. He lived in a house instead of a jail, but he had to be chained to a guard day and night. No doubt many of his guards accepted Christ as their Savior, because Paul never stopped talking about the Lord.

He was encouraged by Christians who visited him every day. Non-believers came, too, to hear the famous apostle tell about the resurrected Son of God, and the salvation He came to provide.

While Paul continued teaching about Jesus in Rome, other men and women were busy carrying the good news about God's gift to every corner of the wide Roman empire, and beyond. And because the believers in the early church were faithful, you have the true message of salvation—today!

It is the responsibility of today's church, and today's Christians, to keep that message alive. "Go ye into all the world and preach the gospel . . ."